90 Arthritis-Preventive Juice and Salad Recipes

The Simple Guide to Naturally Reducing Aches and Pains

By

Joe Correa CSN

COPYRIGHT

© 2019 Live Stronger Faster Inc.

All rights reserved

Reproduction or translation of any part of this work beyond that permitted by section 107 or 108 of the 1976 United States Copyright Act without the permission of the copyright owner is unlawful.

This publication is designed to provide accurate and authoritative information in regard to the subject matter covered. It is sold with the understanding that neither the author nor the publisher is engaged in rendering medical advice. If medical advice or assistance is needed, consult with a doctor. This book is considered a guide and should not be used in any way detrimental to your health. Consult with a physician before starting this nutritional plan to make sure it's right for you.

ACKNOWLEDGEMENTS

This book is dedicated to my friends and family that have had mild or serious illnesses so that you may find a solution and make the necessary changes in your life.

90 Arthritis-Preventive Juice and Salad Recipes

The Simple Guide to Naturally Reducing Aches and Pains

By

Joe Correa CSN

CONTENTS

Copyright

Acknowledgements

About The Author

Introduction

Commitment

90 Arthritis-Preventive Juice and Salad Recipes: The Simple Guide to Naturally Reducing Aches and Pains

Additional Titles from This Author

ABOUT THE AUTHOR

After years of Research, I honestly believe in the positive effects that proper nutrition can have over the body and mind. My knowledge and experience has helped me live healthier throughout the years and which I have shared with family and friends. The more you know about eating and drinking healthier, the sooner you will want to change your life and eating habits.

Nutrition is a key part in the process of being healthy and living longer so get started today. The first step is the most important and the most significant.

INTRODUCTION

90 Arthritis-Preventive Juice and Salad Recipes: The Simple Guide to Naturally Reducing Aches and Pains

By Joe Correa CSN

Early symptoms of arthritis include joint pain, joint swelling, stiffness (especially in the morning), and redness of the skin around the affected joint. In most cases, symptoms don't develop overnight but over a long period of time (months or even years). Other common symptoms most people affected by arthritis often experience loss of appetite, energy loss, slight fever, and red blood cell count decrease. Recognizing the symptoms of arthritis and seeing the physician is an extremely important part of the treatment because both, osteoarthritis and rheumatoid arthritis can cause severe joint deformity if left untreated.

A proper nutrition plays an important role in reducing the risk of arthritis. Our modern diet, based on animal-derived foods, refined sugar, and foods that provoke the immune system response increases the sensitivity for inflammation which leads to this painful disease. With a good nutrition, consistency, and good lifestyle choices, your health will improve significantly and your body will get a chance to resist the inflammation. Furthermore, healthy, fresh, and unprocessed foods will reduce the risk of obesity which not only contributes to the onset and progress of arthritis but also makes your joints carry more weight. Excess weight directly damages your joints and contributes to both - development and progress of this disease.

The main reason I have created this great collection of arthritis preventing recipes was to give you a quick and simple way to get all the nutrients you need in order to boost your immune system, cleanse your body, and lose some weight all at the same time. Juicing is one of the best ways to nourish your body with amazingly valuable antioxidants and other important substances in just a few minutes. This collection of recipes is especially practical for people with busy schedules who have very little to prepare everything. It's also a perfect option for those of you who don't enjoy eating specific fruits or vegetables throughout the day, but still want to get huge amounts of vitamins and minerals into their body.

I hope these powerful recipes will serve as a guide for your arthritis problems. These recipes will make your digestion easier and will help eliminate dangerous toxins that lead to inflammation and arthritis. This book is all about getting the right nutrients you need in a more convenient way and preventing arthritis once and for all. Get started today!

COMMITMENT

In order to improve my condition, I *(your name)*, commit to eating more of these foods on a daily basis and to exercise at least 30 minutes daily:

- Berries (especially blueberries), peaches, cherries, apples, apricots, oranges, lemon juice, grapefruit, tangerines, mandarins, pears, etc.
- Broccoli, spinach, collard greens, sweet potatoes, avocado, artichoke, baby corn, carrots, celery, cauliflower, onions, etc.
- Whole grains, steel-cut oats, oatmeal, quinoa, barley, etc.
- Black beans, red bean beans, garbanzo beans, lentils, etc.
- Nuts and seeds including: walnuts, cashews, flaxseeds, sesame seeds, etc.
- Fish
- 8 – 10 glasses of water

Sign here

X_____

90 ARTHRITIS-PREVENTIVE JUICE AND SALAD RECIPES: THE SIMPLE GUIDE TO NATURALLY REDUCING ACHES AND PAINS

JUICE RECIPES

1.   Cherry Cucumber Juice

Ingredients:

2 cups of fresh cherries, pitted

1 large cucumber, sliced

1 large lemon, peeled

1 medium-sized Granny smith apple, cored

2 oz of water

Preparation:

Using a colander, wash the cherries under cold running water. Cut in half and remove the pits. Set aside.

Wash the cucumber and cut into thick slices. Set aside.

Peel the lemon and cut lengthwise in half. Set aside.

Wash the apple and remove the core. Cut into bite-sized pieces and set aside.

Now, combine cherries, cucumber, lemon, and apple in a juicer and process until juiced. Transfer to serving glasses and stir in the water. Add few ice cubes before serving.

Enjoy!

Nutritional information per serving: Kcal: 296, Protein: 6.6g, Carbs: 88.4g, Fats: 1.4g

2. Orange Apricot Juice

Ingredients:

2 large oranges, peeled

2 large apricots, pitted

1 cup of pomegranate seeds

1 cup of green grapes

1 large lemon, peeled

1 small ginger slice, peeled

Preparation:

Peel the oranges and divide into wedges. Set aside.

Wash the apricots and cut in half. Remove the pits and cut into small pieces. Set aside.

Cut the top of the pomegranate fruit using a sharp knife. Slice down to each of the white membranes inside of the fruit. Pop the seeds into a measuring cup and set aside.

Peel the lemon and cut lengthwise in half. Set aside.

Peel the ginger slice and set aside.

Now, combine oranges, apricots, pomegranate, lemon, and

ginger in a juicer. Process until well juiced and transfer to serving glasses. Refrigerate for 20 minutes before serving.

Nutritional information per serving: Kcal: 294, Protein: 7.2g, Carbs: 88.9g, Fats: 2.3g

3. Blueberry Mint Juice

Ingredients:

1 cup of blueberries

1 cup of fresh mint, torn

1 large red apple, cored

1 large cucumber, sliced

2 oz of coconut water

Preparation:

Place the blueberries in a colander and wash under cold running water. Drain and set aside.

Wash the mint thoroughly and torn with hands. Set aside.

Wash the apple and cut in half. Remove the core and cut into bite-sized pieces. Set aside.

Wash the cucumber and gently peel it. Cut into thin slices and set aside.

Now, combine blueberries, mint, apple, and cucumber in a juicer. Process until juiced and transfer to serving glasses. Stir in the coconut water and refrigerate for 15 minutes, or add some ice before serving.

Enjoy!

Nutritional information per serving: Kcal: 258, Protein: 4.7g, Carbs: 74.6g, Fats: 1.6g

4. Strawberry Mango Juice

Ingredients:

6 large strawberries, chopped

1 cup of mango, peeled and chopped

1 cup of cantaloupe, chopped

1 large cucumber, sliced

2 oz of coconut water

Preparation:

Wash the strawberries and cut into bite-sized pieces. Set aside.

Peel the mango and cut into small chunks. Fill the measuring cup and reserve the rest for later.

Cut the cantaloupe in half and scoop out the seeds. Cut two wedges and peel them. Chop into chunks and fill the measuring cup. Reserve the rest of the cantaloupe in a refrigerator.

Wash the cucumber and cut into thick slices. Set aside.

Now, combine strawberries, mango, cantaloupe, and cucumber in a juicer and process until juiced. Transfer to serving glasses and stir in the coconut water. Refrigerate for 30 minutes before serving.

Enjoy!

Nutritional information per serving: Kcal: 209, Protein: 5.3g, Carbs: 56.6g, Fats: 1.5g

5. Avocado Citrus Juice

Ingredients:

1 cup of avocado, pitted and chopped

1 large cucumber, sliced

1 large lemon, peeled

1 cup of fresh spinach, torn

1 large lime, peeled

1 small ginger knob, peeled

3 oz of water

Preparation:

Peel the avocado and cut in half. Remove the pit and chop into chunks. Set aside.

Wash the cucumber and cut into thick slices. Set aside.

Peel the lemon and lime. Cut lengthwise in half and set aside.

Wash the spinach thoroughly and torn with hands. Set aside.

Peel the ginger knob and set aside.

Now, combine avocado, cucumber, lemon, lime, spinach, and ginger in a juicer. Process until juiced and transfer to serving glasses. Stir in the water and refrigerate for 20 minutes before serving.

Enjoy!

Nutritional information per serving: Kcal: 269, Protein: 6.7g, Carbs: 35g, Fats: 22.6g

6. Artichoke Turmeric Juice

Ingredients:

1 large artichoke, peeled and chopped

1 cup of Brussels sprouts, trimmed

1 large carrot, sliced

1 cup of fresh celery, chopped

1 cup of turnip greens, chopped

1 large green apple, cored

½ tsp of turmeric, ground

2 oz of water

Preparation:

Using a sharp knife, trim off the outer leaves of the artichoke. Cut into small pieces and set aside.

Trim off the outer leaves of the Brussels sprouts and wash them thoroughly. Cut in half and set aside.

Wash the carrot and cut into thin slices. Set aside.

Wash the celery and chop it into bite-sized pieces. Set aside.

Wash the apple and cut in half. Remove the core and cut into bite-sized pieces. Set aside.

Wash the turnip greens thoroughly and torn with hands. Set aside.

Now, combine artichoke, Brussels sprouts, carrot, celery, turnip greens, and apple in a juicer. Process until well juiced and transfer to serving glasses. Stir in the turmeric and water. Add some ice before serving.

Nutritional information per serving: Kcal: 205, Protein: 11.3g, Carbs: 66.7g, Fats: 1.4g

7. Watermelon Orange Juice

Ingredients:

2 cups of watermelon, chopped

1 large orange, peeled

1 cup of raspberries

1 large kiwi, peeled

2 oz coconut water

Preparation:

Cut the watermelon lengthwise. For 2 cups, you will need about 2 large wedges. Peel and cut into chunks. Remove the seeds and set aside. Reserve the rest of the melon for some other juices. Set aside.

Peel the orange and divide into wedges. Set aside.

Wash the raspberries thoroughly under cold running water. Drain and set aside.

Peel the kiwi and cut lengthwise in half. Set aside.

Now, combine watermelon, orange, raspberries, and kiwi in a juicer. Process until juiced and transfer to serving glasses. Stir in the coconut water and refrigerate for 15

minutes before serving.

Nutritional information per serving: Kcal: 232, Protein: 5.8g, Carbs: 71.4g, Fats: 1.8g

8. Salted Beet Tomato Juice

Ingredients:

2 cups of beets, trimmed

1 large Roma tomato, chopped

1 large cucumber, sliced

3 large radishes, trimmed

½ tsp of fresh rosemary, chopped

¼ tsp of sea salt

1 oz of water

Preparation:

Wash the beets and trim off the green parts. Cut into small pieces and set aside.

Wash the tomato and place it in a bowl. Cut into bite-sized pieces and reserve the tomato juice while cutting. Set aside.

Wash the cucumber and cut into thin slices. Set aside.

Wash the radishes and trim off the green ends. Cut in half and set aside.

Now, combine beets, tomato, cucumber, radishes, and rosemary in a juicer. Process until well juiced and transfer to serving glasses. Stir in the salt and water. Refrigerate for 10 minutes before serving.

Enjoy!

Nutritional information per serving: Kcal: 152, Protein: 8.2g, Carbs: 44.9g, Fats: 1.2g

9. Pepper Squash Juice

Ingredients:

3 large red bell peppers, chopped

1 cup of butternut squash, cubed

1 cup of parsnip, sliced

1 tbsp of fresh parsley, chopped

2 oz of water

Preparation:

Wash the red bell peppers and cut lengthwise in half. Remove the seeds and chop into small pieces.

Peel the butternut squash and remove the seeds using a spoon. Cut into small cubes and fill the measuring cup. Reserve the rest of the squash for some other recipe. Wrap in a plastic foil and refrigerate.

Wash the parsnip and peel it. Cut into thin slices and set aside.

Now, combine bell peppers, butternut squash, parsnip, and parsley in a juicer. Process until well juiced and transfer to serving glasses. Stir in the water and add some ice.

Serve immediately.

Nutritional information per serving: Kcal: 238, Protein: 7.9g, Carbs: 70.2g, Fats: 2.1g

10. Papaya Pomegranate Juice

Ingredients:

1 large papaya, peeled and chopped

1 cup of pomegranate seeds

1 large green apple, cored

1 tbsp of fresh mint, chopped

2 oz of water

Preparation:

Peel the papaya and cut lengthwise in half. Scoop out the black seeds and flesh using a spoon. Cut into small chunks and set aside.

Cut the top of the pomegranate fruit using a sharp knife. Slice down to each of the white membranes inside of the fruit. Pop the seeds into a measuring cup and set aside.

Wash the apple and cut in half. Using a sharp knife, remove the core and cut into bite-sized pieces. Set aside.

Now, combine papaya, pomegranate, apple, and mint in a juicer. Process until well juiced and transfer to serving glasses. Stir in the water and refrigerate for 15 minutes before serving.

Nutritional information per serving: Kcal: 438, Protein: 6.1g, Carbs: 129g, Fats: 3.4g

11. Plum Blackberry Juice

Ingredients:

5 large plums, pitted

2 cups of blackberries

1 large lemon, peeled

1 cup of black grapes

1 medium-sized Golden delicious apple, cored

2 oz of water

1 tsp of liquid honey

Preparation:

Wash the plums and cut in half. Remove the pits and cut in small pieces. Set aside.

Wash the blackberries thoroughly under cold running water. Drain and set aside.

Peel the lemon and cut lengthwise in half. Set aside.

Wash the black grapes and set aside.

Wash the apple and cut in half. Remove the core and cut into bite-sized pieces. Set aside.

Now, combine plums, blackberries, lemon, black grapes, and apple in a juicer. Process until well juiced and transfer to serving glasses. Stir in the honey and water. Add some ice and serve immediately.

Enjoy!

Nutritional information per serving: Kcal: 344, Protein: 8g, Carbs: 110g, Fats: 3.1g

12. Pineapple Lime Juice

Ingredients:

1 cup of pineapple chunks

2 large limes, peeled

1 cup of guava, chopped

1 large cucumber, sliced

1 tbsp of fresh basil, chopped

2 oz of water

Preparation:

Cut the top of a pineapple and peel it using a sharp knife. Cut into small chunks and fill the measuring cup. Reserve the rest of the pineapple in a refrigerator.

Peel the limes and cut lengthwise in half. Set aside.

Wash the guava and cut into chunks. Fill the measuring cup and reserve the rest for some other recipe in a refrigerator.

Wash the cucumber and cut into thin slices. Set aside.

Now, combine pineapple, limes, guava, cucumber, and basil in a juicer. Process until well juiced and transfer to serving glasses. Stir in the water and refrigerate for 15

minutes before serving.

Nutritional information per serving: Kcal: 158, Protein: 4.7g, Carbs: 47.9g, Fats: 1.1g

13. Cranberry Pear Juice

Ingredients:

1 cup of cranberries

1 large pear, cored

1 large green apple, cored

3 large strawberries, chopped

1 large orange, peeled

¼ tsp of nutmeg, ground

2 oz of coconut water

Preparation:

Wash the cranberries thoroughly under cold running water. Drain and set aside.

Wash the pear and cut lengthwise in half. Remove the core and cut into bite-sized pieces. Set aside.

Wash the apple and cut in half. Remove the core and cut into bite-sized pieces. Set aside.

Wash the strawberries thoroughly and chop into small pieces. Set aside.

Peel the orange and divide into wedges. Set aside.

Now, combine pear, apple, strawberries, orange, and nutmeg in a juicer. Process until well juiced and transfer to serving glasses. Stir in the water and refrigerate or add some ice before serving.

Nutritional information per serving: Kcal: 158, Protein: 4.7g, Carbs: 47.9g, Fats: 1.1g

14. Carrot Orange Juice

Ingredients:

5 large carrots, peeled

1 large orange, peeled and wedged

1 large lemon, peeled

1 cup of Romaine lettuce, torn

1 large cucumber, sliced

¼ tsp of turmeric, ground

Preparation:

Peel and wash the carrots. Cut into thin slices and set aside.

Peel the orange and divide into wedges. Set aside.

Peel the lemon and cut lengthwise in half. Set aside.

Wash the lettuce thoroughly and torn with hands. Set aside.

Wash the cucumber and cut into thin slices. Set aside.

Now, combine carrots, orange, lemon, lettuce, and cucumber in a juicer. Process until well juiced and transfer to serving glasses. Stir in the turmeric and add some ice before serving. Enjoy!

Nutritional information per serving: Kcal: 232, Protein: 8.2g, Carbs: 74g, Fats: 1.7g

15. Asparagus Collard Greens Juice

Ingredients:

1 cup of asparagus, trimmed

1 cup of collard greens, torn

1 cup of watercress, torn

1 green bell pepper, chopped

1 large cucumber, sliced

2 oz of water

¼ tsp of salt

Preparation:

Wash the asparagus and trim off the woody ends. Cut into bite-sized pieces and fill the measuring cup. Reserve the rest for some other juice.

Combine collard greens and watercress in a colander. Wash thoroughly under cold running water and torn with hands. Set aside.

Wash the bell pepper and lengthwise in half. Remove the seeds and chop into small pieces. Set aside.

Wash the cucumber and cut into thin slices. Set aside.

Now, combine asparagus, collard greens, bell pepper, and cucumber in a juicer and process until well juiced. Transfer to serving glasses and stir in the salt and water. Refrigerate for 15 minutes before serving.

Nutritional information per serving: Kcal: 86, Protein: 8.2g, Carbs: 26.1g, Fats: 1g

16. Sweet Potato Green Smoothie

Ingredients:

1 cup of sweet potatoes, peeled

1 large fennel, chopped

1 cup of Swiss chard, torn

1 cup of red leaf lettuce, torn

1 cup of fresh spinach, torn

1 small cauliflower head, chopped

1 large lemon, peeled

Preparation:

Peel the sweet potato and cut into small chunks. Fill the measuring cup and reserve the rest for some other juice.

Wash the fennel bulb and trim off the wilted outer layers. Cut into small chunks and set aside.

Combine Swiss chard, red leaf lettuce, and spinach in a colander. Wash under cold running water and drain. Torn with hands and set aside.

Trim off the outer leaves of cauliflower. Wash it and cut into small pieces. Set aside.

Peel the lemon and cut lengthwise in half. Set aside.

Now, combine potato, fennel, Swiss chard, cauliflower, and lemon in a juicer and process until well juiced. Transfer to serving glasses and add some ice before serving.

Nutritional information per serving: Kcal: 218, Protein: 14.3g, Carbs: 67.7g, Fats: 1.9g

17. Fennel Brussels Sprouts Juice

Ingredients:

1 medium-sized fennel bulb, chopped

1 cup of Brussels sprouts, halved

1 large yellow bell pepper, chopped

1 large cucumber, sliced

¼ tsp of salt

2 oz of water

Preparation:

Trim off the fennel stalks and wilted outer layers. Cut into bite-sized pieces and set aside. Trim off the outer leaves and wash the Brussels sprouts. Cut in half and set aside. Wash the bell pepper and cut lengthwise in half. Remove the seeds and chop into small pieces. Set aside. Wash the cucumber and cut into thin slices. Set aside. Now, combine fennel, Brussels sprouts, bell peppers, and cucumber in a juicer. Process until well juiced and stir in the salt and water. Refrigerate for 10 minutes before serving.

Nutritional information per serving: Kcal: 151, Protein: 9.7g, Carbs: 47.6g, Fats: 1.4g

18. Watermelon Peach Juice

Ingredients:

1 cup of watermelon, cubed

2 large peaches, pitted

1 large green apple, cored

5 fresh cherries, pitted

3 oz of coconut water

Preparation:

Cut the watermelon lengthwise. For one cup, you will need about one large wedge. Peel and cut into chunks. Remove the seeds and set aside. Reserve the rest of the melon for some other juices.

Wash the peaches and cut in half. Remove the pits and cut into bite-sized pieces. Set aside.

Wash the apple and cut in half. Remove the core and cut into bite-sized pieces. Set aside.

Wash the cherries and cut in half. Remove the pits and set aside.

Now, process watermelon, peaches, apple, and cherries in

a juicer. Transfer to serving glasses and stir in the coconut water. Add some ice and serve immediately.

Nutritional information per serving: Kcal: 276, Protein: 5.4g, Carbs: 47.6g, Fats: 1.6g

19. Spinach Apple Juice

Ingredients:

1 cup of fresh spinach, torn

1 large red apple, cored

1 cup of wild asparagus, trimmed

1 cup of collard greens, torn

1 cup of mustard greens, torn

2 oz of water

Preparation:

Combine spinach, collard greens, and mustard greens in a large colander. Wash under cold running water and drain. Torn with hands and set aside. Wash the apple and cut in half. Remove the core and cut into bite-sized pieces. Set aside. Now, combine spinach, collard greens, mustard greens, and apple in a juicer and process until well juiced. Transfer to serving glasses and stir in the water. Refrigerate for 15 minutes before serving. Enjoy!

Nutritional information per serving: Kcal: 207, Protein: 16.1g, Carbs: 58.6g, Fats: 2.5g

20. Plum Cabbage Juice

Ingredients:

5 large plums, pitted

1 cup of purple cabbage, chopped

1 cup of blackberries

1 large cucumber, sliced

2 oz of water

Preparation:

Wash the plums and cut in half. Remove the pits and cut into quarters. Set aside.

Wash the cabbage thoroughly under cold running water. Drain and roughly chop it. Set aside. Wash the blackberries under cold running water using a colander. Slightly drain and set aside. Wash the cucumber and cut into thin slices. Set aside. Now, combine plums, cabbage, blackberries, and cucumber in a juicer and process until juice. Transfer to serving glasses and stir in the water. Refrigerate for 15 minutes before serving.

Nutritional information per serving: Kcal: 221, Protein: 7.5g, Carbs: 69.1g, Fats: 2.1g

21. Crookneck Squash Tomato Juice

Ingredients:

1 cup of crookneck squash, chopped

1 large tomato, chopped

1 large lemon, peeled

1 large orange, peeled

1 large pear, cored and chopped

2 oz of water

1 tsp of liquid honey

Preparation:

Wash the crookneck squash and cut in half. Scoop out the seeds using a spoon. Cut into small chunks and fill the measuring cup. Reserve the rest for another juice.

Wash the tomato and place it in a bowl. Cut into bite-sized pieces and reserve the juice while cutting. Set aside.

Peel the lemon and cut lengthwise in half. Set aside.

Peel the orange and divide into wedges. Set aside.

Wash the pear and cut lengthwise in half. Remove the core

and cut into bite-sized pieces. Set aside.

Now, combine crookneck squash, tomato, lemon, orange, and pear in a juicer. Process until well juiced and transfer to serving glasses. Stir in the water and honey. Add some ice and serve immediately.

Nutritional information per serving: Kcal: 201, Protein: 5.9g, Carbs: 66.1g, Fats: 1.3g

22. Cauliflower Leek Juice

Ingredients:

1 small cauliflower head, chopped

3 large leeks, chopped

1 large lime, peeled

1 large zucchini, chopped

2 oz of water

Preparation:

Trim off the outer leaves of cauliflower. Wash it and cut into small pieces. Set aside. Wash the leeks and cut into small pieces. Set aside. Peel the lime and cut lengthwise in half. Set aside. Peel the zucchini and cut in half. Scrape out the seeds and cut into small chunks. Set aside.

Now, combine cauliflower, leeks, lime, and zucchini in a juicer. Process until well juiced and stir in the water. Refrigerate for 10 minutes before serving.

Enjoy!

Nutritional information per serving: Kcal: 241, Protein: 13.2g, Carbs: 64.7g, Fats: 2.6g

23. Raspberry Beet Juice

Ingredients:

2 cups of raspberries

1 large green apple, cored

1 cup of beets, chopped

1 cup of fresh basil, torn

1 large lemon, peeled

3 oz of water

Preparation:

Wash the raspberries under cold running water using a colander. Drain and set aside.

Wash the apple and cut in half. Remove the core and cut into bite-sized pieces. Set aside.

Wash the beets and trim off the green ends. Cut into small pieces and fill the measuring cup. Reserve the greens for some other juice.

Wash the basil thoroughly under cold running water and torn with hands. Set aside.

Peel the lemon and cut lengthwise in half. Set aside.

Now, combine raspberries, apple, beets, basil, and lemon in a juicer. Process until well juiced. Stir in the water and refrigerate for 10 minutes before serving.

Enjoy!

Nutritional information per serving: Kcal: 218, Protein: 7.5g, Carbs: 76.4g, Fats: 2.5g

24. Apricot Pomegranate Juice

Ingredients:

1 large apricot, pitted

1 cup of pomegranate seeds

1 large lemon, peeled

1 large orange, wedged

1 large carrot, peeled

2 oz of coconut water

Preparation:

Wash the apricot and cut in half. Remove the pit and cut into small pieces. Set aside.

Cut the top of the pomegranate fruit using a sharp knife. Slice down to each of the white membranes inside of the fruit. Pop the seeds into measuring cup and set aside.

Peel the lemon and cut lengthwise in half. Set aside.

Peel the orange and divide into wedges. Set aside.

Peel and wash the carrot. Cut into thin slices and set aside.

Now, combine apricot, pomegranate seeds, lemon, orange,

and carrot in a juicer. Process until well juiced and transfer to serving glasses. Stir in the coconut water and add few ice cubes before serving.

Nutritional information per serving: Kcal: 241, Protein: 7.3g, Carbs: 73.9g, Fats: 2.3g

25. Broccoli Kale Juice

Ingredients:

2 cups of broccoli, trimmed

1 cup of fresh kale, torn

1 cup of fresh parsley, torn

1 large green apple, chopped

1 cup of fresh spinach, torn

2 oz of water

Preparation:

Wash the broccoli under cold running water and cut into small pieces. Set aside. Combine parsley, kale, and spinach in a colander and wash under cold running water. Drain and torn with hands. Set aside. Wash the apple and cut in half. Remove the core and cut into bite-sized pieces. Set aside.

Now, combine broccoli, kale, parsley, apple, and spinach in a juicer. Process until well juiced and stir in the water.

Refrigerate for 20 minutes before serving.

Nutritional information per serving: Kcal: 223, Protein: 20.4g, Carbs: 62.1g, Fats: 3.5g

26. Mango Cherry Juice

Ingredients:

1 cup of mango, chopped

1 cup of fresh cherries, pitted

2 cup of green grapes

1 large lemon, peeled

2 oz of water

Preparation:

Wash the mango and cut into chunks. Fill the measuring cup and reserve the rest for some other juice. Set aside.

Wash the cherries and cut in half. Remove the pits and set aside. Wash the grapes and fill the measuring cup. Reserve the rest for some other juice. Set aside. Peel the lemon and cut lengthwise in half. Set aside. Now, combine mango, cherries, grapes, and lemon in a juicer and process until well juiced. Transfer to serving glasses and stir in the water.

Add few ice cubes and serve immediately.

Nutritional information per serving: Kcal: 302, Protein: 4.8g, Carbs: 86.3g, Fats: 1.7g

27. Grapefruit Apple Juice

Ingredients:

2 large grapefruits, peeled

1 large red apple, cored

2 large strawberries, chopped

1 small ginger knob, peeled

2 oz of coconut water

Preparation:

Peel the grapefruits and divide into wedges. Set aside.

Wash the apple and cut in half. Remove the core and cut into bite-sized pieces. Set aside.

Wash the strawberries and cut into small pieces. Set aside.

Peel the ginger knob and set aside.

Now, combine grapefruits, apple, strawberries, and ginger in a juicer. Process until well juiced and transfer to serving glasses. Stir in the coconut water and refrigerate for 15 minutes, or add some ice before serving.

Nutritional information per serving: Kcal: 302, Protein: 4.8g, Carbs: 86.3g, Fats: 1.7g

28. Pumpkin Nutmeg Juice

Ingredients:

2 cups of pumpkin, cubed

1 large green apple, cored

1 large cucumber, sliced

1 cup of Swiss chard, torn

2 oz of water

¼ tsp of nutmeg, ground

Preparation:

Peel the pumpkin and cut in half. Scoop out the seeds using a spoon. Cut one large wedge and peel it. Cut into small cubes and fill the measuring cup. Reserve the rest for some other juice.

Wash the apple and cut in half. Remove the core and cut into bite-sized pieces. Set aside.

Wash the cucumber and cut into thin slices. Set aside.

Wash the Swiss chard thoroughly under cold running water. Drain and torn with hands. Set aside.

Now, combine pumpkin, apple, cucumber, and Swiss

chards in a juicer. Process until well juiced and stir in the water and nutmeg. Refrigerate for 15 minutes before serving.

Nutritional information per serving: Kcal: 196, Protein: 5.8g, Carbs: 55.4g, Fats: 1.1g

29. Celery Green Bean Juice

Ingredients:

2 cups of celery, chopped

1 cup of green beans, chopped

1 cup of fresh mint, torn

1 cup of beet greens, torn

1 large cucumber, sliced

2 oz of water

¼ tsp of salt

Preparation:

Wash the celery and cut into small pieces. Set aside.

Wash the green beans and cut into bite-sized pieces. Set aside.

Combine mint and beet greens in a colander. Wash under cold running water and torn with hands. Set aside.

Wash the cucumber and cut into thin slices. Set aside.

Now, combine celery, green beans, mint, beet greens, and cucumber in a juicer. Process until well juiced and transfer to serving glasses. Stir in the water and salt.

Refrigerate for 10 minutes before serving.

Nutritional information per serving: Kcal: 91, Protein: 6.1g, Carbs: 26.1g, Fats: 1g

30. Strawberry Peach Juice

Ingredients:

1 cup of strawberries, chopped

2 large peaches, pitted

1 large green apple, cored

1 large lemon, peeled

1 large kiwi, peeled

1 large orange, peeled

2 oz of water

Preparation:

Wash the strawberries under cold running water. Remove the green parts and cut into bite-sized pieces. Set aside.

Wash the peaches and cut in half. Remove the pits and cut into small pieces. Set aside.

Wash the apple and cut half. Remove the core and cut into bite-sized pieces. Set aside.

Peel the lemon and kiwi. Cut lengthwise in half and set aside.

Now, combine strawberries, peaches, apple, lemon, and kiwi in a juicer and process until well juiced. Transfer to serving glasses and stir in the water. Add some ice and serve immediately.

Enjoy!

Nutritional information per serving: Kcal: 345, Protein: 7.8g, Carbs: 105g, Fats: 2.3g

31. Sour Pepper Lemon Juice

Ingredients:

1 large red bell pepper, chopped

1 large lemon, peeled

1 cup of beets, chopped

1 large cucumber, sliced

1 tsp of balsamic vinegar

¼ tsp of salt

2 oz of water

Preparation:

Wash the bell pepper and cut in half. Remove the seeds and chop into small pieces. Set aside.

Peel the lemon and cut lengthwise in half. Set aside.

Wash the beets and trim off the green ends. Cut into bite-sized pieces and fill the measuring cup. Reserve the rest for some other juice. Set aside.

Wash the cucumber and cut into thin slices. Set aside.

Now, combine bell pepper, lemon, beets, and cucumber in

a juicer. Process until well juiced and transfer to serving glasses. Stir in the balsamic vinegar, salt, and water.

Refrigerate for 20 minutes before serving.

Nutritional information per serving: Kcal: 130, Protein: 6.4g, Carbs: 39.2g, Fats: 1.2g

32. Blackberry Apricot Juice

Ingredients:

1 cup of blackberries

1 cup of raspberries

3 large apricots, pitted

1 large red apple, cored

3 large carrots, peeled

Preparation:

Combine blackberries and raspberries in a colander. Wash under cold running water and slightly drain. Set aside.

Wash the apricots and cut in half. Remove the pits and cut into bite-sized pieces. Set aside.

Wash the apple and cut in half. Remove the core and cut into small pieces.

Wash and peel the carrots. Cut into thin slices and set aside.

Now, combine blackberries, raspberries, apricots, apple, and carrots in a juicer. Process until well juiced and transfer to serving glasses. Stir in the water and refrigerate for 20

minutes before serving.

Enjoy!

Nutritional information per serving: Kcal: 301, Protein: 7.6g, Carbs: 97.4g, Fats: 2.9g

33. Strawberry Avocado Juice

Ingredients:

5 large strawberries, chopped

1 cup of avocado, pitted

1 cup of fresh mint, chopped

1 large apple, cored

1 large lemon, peeled

1 large cucumber, sliced

Preparation:

Wash the strawberries and cut into small pieces. Set aside.

Peel the avocado and cut lengthwise in half. Remove the pit and cut into chunks and fill the measuring cup. Reserve the rest for later.

Wash the mint thoroughly and torn with hands. Set aside.

Wash the apple and cut in half. Remove the core and cut into bite-sized pieces. Set aside.

Peel the lemon and cut lengthwise in half. Set aside.

Wash the cucumber and cut into thin slices. Set aside.

Now, combine strawberries, avocado, mint, lemon, and cucumber in a juicer and process until juiced. Transfer to serving glasses and stir in the water. Add some ice and serve immediately.

Nutritional information per serving: Kcal: 376, Protein: 8.1g, Carbs: 67.8g, Fats: 23.3g

34. Cantaloupe Carrot Juice

Ingredients:

1 cup of cantaloupe, cubed

3 large carrots, sliced

1 large orange, peeled

1 large green apple, cored

2 oz of coconut water

Preparation:

Cut the cantaloupe in half. Scoop out the seeds and flesh. Cut two wedges and peel them. Chop into cubes and set aside. Reserve the rest of the cantaloupe in a refrigerator.

Wash and peel the carrots. Cut into thin slices and set aside.

Peel the orange and divide into wedges. Set aside.

Wash the apple and cut in half. Remove the core and cut into bite-sized pieces. Set aside.

Now, combine cantaloupe, carrots, orange, and apple in a juicer. Process until well juiced and stir in the coconut water.

Nutritional information per serving: Kcal: 277, Protein: 6g, Carbs: 83g, Fats: 1.4g

35. Pomegranate Pepper Juice

Ingredients:

1 cup of pomegranate seeds

1 large red bell pepper, chopped

1 cup of cranberries

4 large plums, pitted

1 large green apple, cored

Preparation:

Cut the top of the pomegranate fruit using a sharp knife. Slice down to each of the white membranes inside of the fruit. Pop the seeds into a measuring cup and set aside.

Wash the bell pepper and cut lengthwise in half. Remove the seeds and cut into small pieces. Set aside.

Wash the cranberries thoroughly and drain. Set aside.

Wash the plums and cut in half. Remove the pits and cut into bite-sized pieces. Set aside.

Wash the apple and cut in half. Remove the core and cut into bite-sized pieces. Set aside.

Now, combine pomegranate, cranberries, plums, and

apple in a juicer. Process until well juiced and add some ice before serving.

Enjoy!

Nutritional information per serving: Kcal: 277, Protein: 6g, Carbs: 83g, Fats: 1.4g

36. Zucchini Kiwi Juice

Ingredients:

1 large zucchini, seeded

3 large kiwis, peeled

1 large lime, peeled

1 cup of pomegranate seeds

1 large orange, peeled

Preparation:

Wash the zucchini and cut in half. Scoop out the seeds using a spoon. Cut into small chunks and set aside.

Peel the kiwis and lime. Cut lengthwise in half and set aside.

Cut the top of the pomegranate fruit using a sharp knife. Slice down to each of the white membranes inside of the fruit. Pop the seeds into a measuring cup and set aside.

Peel the orange and divide into wedges. Set aside.

Now, process kiwis, zucchini, lime, pomegranate seeds, and orange in a juicer.

Transfer to a serving glasses and add some ice cubes before serving.

Nutritional information per serving: Kcal: 183, Protein: 8.5g, Carbs: 52.6g, Fats: 1.6g

37. Blueberry Mango Juice

Ingredients:

1 cup of mango, chopped

1 cup of blueberries

1 large cucumber, sliced

1 large green apple, cored

2 oz of water

Preparation:

Wash the mango and cut into chunks. Fill the measuring cup and reserve the rest for some other juice. Set aside.

Place the blueberries in a colander and wash under cold running water. Drain and set aside.

Wash the apple and remove the core. Cut into bite-sized pieces and set aside.

Now, combine mango, blueberries, and apple in a juicer and process until juiced.

Transfer to serving glasses and stir in the water. Add some ice before serving and enjoy!

Nutritional information per serving: Kcal: 180, Protein: 5.9g, Carbs: 63.5g, Fats: 1.1g

38. Carrot Lemon Juice

Ingredients:

5 large carrots, sliced

2 large lemons, peeled

1 large green apple, cored

1 cup of Romaine lettuce

2 oz of water

Preparation:

Wash the carrots and cut into thick slices. Set aside.

Peel the lemons and cut lengthwise in half. Set aside.

Wash the apple and remove the core. Cut into bite-sized pieces and set aside.

Wash the lettuce thoroughly under cold running water. Torn with hands and set aside.

Now, process carrots, lettuce, lemon, and apple in a juicer. Transfer to serving glasses and add some ice before serving.

Enjoy!

Nutritional information per serving: Kcal: 232, Protein: 6.1g, Carbs: 74.9g, Fats: 1.7g

39. Guava Lime Juice

Ingredients:

1 large guava, peeled

1 large lime, peeled

2 large oranges, peeled

1 large cucumber, sliced

2 oz of water

Preparation:

Peel and wash the guava. Cut into small chunks and set aside.

Peel the lime and cut lengthwise in half. Set aside.

Peel the oranges and divide into wedges. Set aside.

Wash the cucumber and cut into thin slices. Set aside.

Now, combine lime, guava, orange, and cucumber in a juicer and process until juiced.

Transfer to serving glasses and stir in the water. Add some ice and serve immediately.

Nutritional information per serving: Kcal: 210, Protein: 7g, Carbs: 65.7g, Fats: 1.3g

40. Celery Lemon Juice

Ingredients:

1 large lemon, peeled

1 cup of celery, chopped

1 cup of fresh mint, chopped

1 cup of fresh spinach, chopped

2 oz of water

Preparation:

Peel the lemon and cut lengthwise in half. Set aside.

Wash the celery stalks and chop into small pieces. Fill the measuring cup and set aside.

Wash the spinach and mint in a colander. Chop and place in a medium bowl. Set aside.

Now, combine lemon, celery, mint, and spinach in a juicer and process until juiced. Transfer to serving glasses and stir in the water.

Refrigerate for 10 minutes before serving.

Nutritional information per serving: Kcal: 35, Protein: 3.1g, Carbs: 13.2g, Fats: 0.7g

41. Basil Lemon Juice

Ingredients:

1 cup of fresh basil, chopped

1 large lemon, peeled

1 cup of Swiss chard, chopped

1 large green apple, cored

1 cup of fresh mint, chopped

2 oz of water

Preparation:

Combine basil, Swiss chard, and mint in a large colander. Wash thoroughly under cold running water. Chop into small pieces and set aside. Peel the lemon and cut lengthwise in half. Wash the apple and cut in half. Remove the core and cut into bite-sized pieces. Set aside. Now, combine basil, Swiss chard, mint, lemon, and apple in a juicer and process until well juiced. Transfer to serving glasses and stir in the water.

Refrigerate for 10 minutes before serving.

Nutritional information per serving: Kcal: 126, Protein: 3.9g, Carbs: 39.1g, Fats: 1.1g

42. Pineapple Carrot Juice

Ingredients:

1 cup of pineapple chunks

2 large carrots, sliced

1 cup of watercress, torn

1 large lime, peeled

1 small ginger knob, peeled

2 oz of water

Preparation:

Peel the pineapple and cut into small chunks. Set aside.

Wash and peel the carrots. Cut into thin slices and set aside.

Wash the watercress thoroughly under cold running water. Torn with hands and set aside.

Peel the lime and cut lengthwise in half. Set aside.

Peel the ginger root knob and cut into small pieces. Set aside.

Now, combine pineapple, carrots, watercress, lemon, and

ginger in a juicer and process until well juiced.

Transfer to serving glasses and stir in water.

Add some ice and serve.

Nutritional information per serving: Kcal: 135, Protein: 3.3g, Carbs: 40.6g, Fats: 3.3g

43. Orange Apple Juice

Ingredients:

3 large oranges, peeled

1 large green apple, cored

1 cup of fresh asparagus, trimmed

¼ tsp of turmeric, ground

2 oz of water

Preparation:

Peel the oranges and divide into wedges. Set aside.

Wash the apple and remove the core. Cut into bite-sized pieces and set aside.

Wash the asparagus thoroughly under cold running water and trim off the woody ends. Cut into small pieces and set aside.

Now, combine oranges, apple, and asparagus in a juicer and process until juiced. Transfer to serving glasses and stir in the turmeric and water.

Refrigerate for 10 minutes before serving.

Nutritional information per serving: Kcal: 316, Protein: 9.1g, Carbs: 98.1g, Fats: 1.2g

SALAD RECIPES

1. Smoked Salmon Salad

Ingredients:

4 oz. smoked salmon, sliced

½ red onion, sliced

1 cup Iceberg lettuce, roughly chopped

¼ cup Feta cheese, crumbled

¼ cup Kalamata olives, pitted

1 tbsp. extra-virgin olive oil

¼ tsp. garlic powder

½ tsp. dried thyme

¼ tsp. dried rosemary

¼ tsp. sea salt

¼ tsp. black pepper, ground

Preparation:

In a small bowl, combine olive oil, garlic powder, thyme,

rosemary, salt, and pepper. Stir until well combined and set aside.

Rinse and drain the lettuce. Roughly chop and place in a large bowl. Top with onions, salmon, and cheese.

Drizzle with previously prepared dressing and serve immediately.

Optionally, sprinkle with some fresh lemon juice for some extra taste.

Enjoy!

Nutritional information per serving: Kcal: 213, Protein: 13.7g, Carbs: 5.9g, Fats: 15.4g

2. Spinach Mushroom Salad

Ingredients:

4 cups fresh spinach, rinsed

2 cups button mushrooms

1 medium-sized red onion, thinly sliced

3 tbsp. olive oil

1 tsp. coconut sugar

¼ cup balsamic vinegar

½ tsp. salt

¼ tsp. black pepper, ground

Preparation:

In a small skillet, combine balsamic vinegar, coconut sugar, salt, and pepper. Bring it to a boil and remove from the heat immediately. Let it chill completely and then add sliced onions. Cover with a lid and refrigerate for later.

Now, preheat the oil in a large skillet over medium-high heat. Add mushrooms and sprinkle with some salt and pepper to taste. Cook for 10 minutes, stirring occasionally.

Add one cup of spinach to the skillet and cook for 1-2

minutes, or until the spinach has been wilted. Remove from the heat and set aside.

Arrange the remaining spinach on a serving plate and top with mushroom and spinach mixture. Add onions and remaining marinade.

Serve immediately.

Nutritional information per serving: Kcal: 243, Protein: 4.6g, Carbs: 11.5g, Fats: 21.5g

3. Green Bean Salad with Baby Potatoes

Ingredients:

2 cups fresh green beans

1 cup baby potatoes, peeled

1 small red onion, sliced

3 tbsp. olive oil

2 tsp. yellow mustard

1 tsp. fresh thyme, finely chopped

2 tsp. lemon juice, freshly squeezed

¼ tsp. salt

¼ tsp. black pepper

Preparation:

In a small mixing bowl, combine olive oil, yellow mustard, thyme, lemon juice, salt, and pepper. Mix until well combined and set aside.

Place the green beans in a deep pot and add water enough to cover. Sprinkle with some salt and bring it to a simmer. Cook for 2-3 minutes, or until almost tender. Remove from the heat. Using a large mesh skimmer, transfer to a large bowl and set aside.

Place the potatoes to the same pot and bring it to a boil over medium-high heat. Simmer for 10-12 minutes, or until fork-tender. Remove from the heat and drain. Cut into bite-sized pieces and add to the bowl with green beans.

Add onions and drizzle all with previously prepared dressing. Gently toss until well incorporated and serve immediately.

Nutritional information per serving: Kcal: 246, Protein: 3.2g, Carbs: 14.3g, Fats: 21.5g

4. Frisee Arugula Salad

Ingredients:

3 cups fresh frisee, torn

2 cups arugula, torn

1 tbsp. lemon juice, freshly squeezed

1 tsp. Dijon mustard

1 tbsp. olive oil

½ tsp. salt

¼ tsp. black pepper, ground

½ tsp. Italian seasoning

Preparation:

Combine all greens in a large colander. Rinse under cold running water and drain. Chop into bite-sized pieces and transfer to a large bowl. Set aside.

In a small bowl, combine lemon juice, Dijon mustard, olive oil, salt, pepper and Italian seasoning. Mix until well combined and drizzle over the salad.

You can add some more greens of your choice, such as spinach, kale, or watercress. However, it's optional.

Serve immediately.

Nutritional information per serving: Kcal: 246, Protein: 3.2g, Carbs: 14.3g, Fats: 21.5g

5. Sweet Buckwheat Salad with Avocado and Spinach

Ingredients:

1 cup buckwheat groats

½ ripe avocado, peeled and sliced

1 cup fresh spinach, rinsed and chopped

½ medium-sized cucumber, sliced

½ cup black beans, soaked overnight

1 whole lime, juiced

1 tbsp. olive oil

1 tsp. maple syrup

¼ tsp. cumin powder

¼ tsp. cayenne pepper

Salt and pepper to taste

Preparation:

Place the buckwheat in a heavy-bottomed pot and add 2 cups of water. Bring it to a boil over medium-high heat. Cook for 10-15 minutes, or until tender. Remove from the heat and drain the excess liquid. Set aside.

Drain the beans and place them in a pot. Add water enough to cover all and bring it to a boil. Cook for 30 minutes. Remove from the heat and drain. Set aside.

Using a large colander, rinse the spinach under cold running water. Drain and transfer to a large bowl. Add cooked buckwheat, cooked beans, avocado, and sliced cucumber.

In a small bowl, combine olive oil, lime juice, maple syrup, cumin powder, cayenne pepper, salt, and pepper. Stir well until combined and drizzle over the salad.

Serve immediately.

Nutritional information per serving: Kcal: 287, Protein: 10.2g, Carbs: 38.1g, Fats: 12.2g

6. Fried Red Bell Pepper Salad

Ingredients:

5 medium-sized red bell peppers, halved lengthwise and seeds removed

1 garlic clove, minced

1 tbsp. capers, drained

¼ cup olives, pitted

1 tbsp. balsamic vinegar

2 tbsp. extra-virgin olive oil

1 tbsp. fresh parsley, finely chopped

1 tsp. sea salt

Preparation:

In a small bowl, combine garlic, capers, olives, balsamic vinegar, parsley, salt, and one tablespoon of oil. Stir well and set aside for 15 minutes before use.

Grease a large non-stick pan with the remaining olive oil. Heat up over medium-high heat. Add bell peppers and sprinkle with some salt. Cook for 5 minutes, or until tender and brown on the edges. Remove from the heat and transfer to a large bowl.

Top with previously prepared mixture and sprinkle with finely chopped parsley before serving.

Nutritional information per serving: Kcal: 240, Protein: 3.4g, Carbs: 24.5g, Fats: 16.6g

7. Cheesy Chicken Salad

Ingredients:

1 lb. chicken breast, skinless and boneless

¼ cup cottage cheese, crumbled

1 medium-sized red bell pepper, chopped

1 small cucumber, sliced

1 small red onion, chopped

2 cups Romaine lettuce, chopped

1 tsp. lemon juice, freshly squeezed

1 tsp. Worcestershire sauce

1 tbsp. olive oil

½ tsp. dried thyme, ground

¼ tsp. smoked paprika

¼ tsp. garlic powder

Salt to taste

Preparation:

Rinse well the chicken and pat-dry with a kitchen paper.

Transfer to cutting board and cut into bite-sized pieces. Set aside.

Preheat the oil in a saucepan over medium-high heat. Add chicken and sprinkle with garlic powder, thyme, smoked paprika, and salt to taste. Cook for 5-7 minutes, or until golden brown. Remove from the heat and set aside.

Rinse the lettuce under cold running water. Chop into bite-sized pieces and place in large bowl along with cottage cheese, cucumber, bell pepper, and onion.

Sprinkle all with Worcestershire sauce and lemon juice. Give it a good stir and serve immediately.

Nutritional information per serving: Kcal: 275, Protein: 36.2g, Carbs: 11.4g, Fats: 9.2g

8.   Sweet Potato Salad with Eggs

Ingredients:

2 medium-sized sweet potatoes

2 eggs

1 medium-sized onion, sliced

1 tbsp. olive oil

1 tbsp. fresh parsley, finely chopped

½ tsp. salt

½ tsp. black pepper, ground

¼ tsp. dried oregano, ground

¼ tsp. dried rosemary, ground

Preparation:

Place the eggs in a deep pot and add enough water to cover. Bring it to a boil and cook for 10 minutes. Remove from the heat and transfer immediately to ice cold water. Let it chill for a few minutes. Peel and cut into bite-sized pieces. Set aside.

Peel the potatoes and cut into bite-sized cubes.

Peel the onion and cut into thin slices. Set aside.

Place the sweet potatoes in a heavy-bottomed pot and cover with water. Bring it to a boil and cook for 7-10 minutes over a medium-high heat. Remove from the heat and drain well.

Preheat the oil in a large saucepan over medium-high heat. Add potatoes and sprinkle with salt, pepper, oregano, and rosemary. Cook for 2-3 minutes and remove from the heat.

Transfer the potatoes to a large bowl along with eggs, onion, and parsley. Stir until well incorporated.

Nutritional information per serving: Kcal: 217, Protein: 5.7g, Carbs: 32g, Fats: 7.9g

9. Greek Style Salad

Ingredients:

2 large tomatoes, chopped

¼ cup Feta cheese, crumbled

1 cucumber, sliced

1 medium-sized capsicum, chopped

1 small onion, chopped

¼ cup black olives, pitted

1 tbsp. olive oil

½ tsp. salt

½ tsp. black pepper, ground

Preparation:

Rinse the tomatoes and transfer to a cutting board. Cut into bite-sized pieces and set aside.

Wash the cucumber and cut into thin slices. Set aside.

Peel the onion and chop into small pieces. Place in a small bowl and add water enough to cover. Sprinkle with some salt and mix. Let it soak for 10 minutes. When done, drain and squeeze with your hands to remove the excess water.

Wash the pepper and cut lengthwise into halves. Remove the stem and seeds. Chop into small pieces and set aside.

Now, combine all prepared ingredients in a large bowl. Add olives and sprinkle all with olive oil, salt, and pepper to taste. Give it a good stir and serve immediately.

Nutritional information per serving: Kcal: 209, Protein: 6.3g, Carbs: 20g, Fats: 13.5g

10. Cabbage Radish Salad

Ingredients:

2 cups cabbage, shredded

2 medium-sized radishes, thinly sliced

1 medium-sized purple onion, sliced

2 eggs

1 tbsp. olive oil

1 tbsp. white wine vinegar

1 tsp. Italian seasoning

¼ tsp. black pepper, ground

Preparation:

Wash the radishes and trim off the green parts. Using a sharp knife, cut into thin slices and set aside.

Peel the onion and cut into thin slices. Sprinkle with some salt and set aside.

In a small mixing bowl, combine olive oil, vinegar, Italian seasoning, and pepper. Mix until well combined and set aside.

Place the eggs in a deep pot. Add water enough to cover and bring it to a boil over medium-high heat. Cook for 10 minutes and remove from the heat. Let it cool completely. Peel and cut into bite-sized pieces.

Now, combine cabbage, radishes, onion, and eggs in a large bowl. Drizzle with previously prepared dressing and serve immediately.

Nutritional information per serving: Kcal: 173, Protein: 7.1g, Carbs: 10.2g, Fats: 12.2g

11. Mediterranean Salad

Ingredients:

4 oz. shrimps, cleaned and deveined

1 cup cherry tomatoes, halved

1 medium-sized purple onion, sliced

1 green bell pepper, chopped

¼ cup green olives, pitted

½ ripe avocado, sliced

¼ cup goat's cheese crumbled

2 tbsp. olive oil

1 tsp. balsamic vinegar

½ tsp. sea salt

¼ tsp. dried thyme, ground

¼ tsp. dried oregano, ground

¼ tsp. black pepper

Preparation:

Preheat one tablespoon of olive oil in a large non-stick

skillet over medium-high heat. Add shrimps and sprinkle with some salt and pepper. Cook for 2-3 minutes on each side. Remove from the heat and set aside.

In a small mixing bowl, combine the remaining olive oil, balsamic vinegar, thyme, and oregano. Mix until combined and set aside.

Wash and prepare the vegetables.

Now, combine shrimps, cherry tomatoes, purple onion, green bell pepper, and olives in a large salad bowl. Drizzle all with previously prepared dressing and gently toss.

Finally top with cheese and avocado slices and serve immediately.

Enjoy!

Nutritional information per serving: Kcal: 304, Protein: 14.8g, Carbs: 13.9g, Fats: 22.4g

12. Rice Vegetable Salad

Ingredients:

½ cup brown rice, long-grain

2 tbsp. olive oil

½ cup cherry tomatoes, halved

1 small cucumber, cut into bite-sized cubes

2 oz. Feta cheese, crumbled

½ tbsp. sherry vinegar

1 small onion, finely chopped

1 garlic clove, minced

½ cup fresh mint, roughly chopped

½ cup fresh parsley, roughly chopped

Salt and pepper to taste

Preparation:

Preheat one tablespoon of olive oil in a saucepan over medium-high heat. Add minced garlic and finely chopped onions. Sprinkle with some salt and stir-fry for 3-4 minutes, or until translucent. Remove the mixture from the pan and set aside.

Add the remaining oil to the pan and heat up over medium-high heat. Add rice and fry for 2 minutes, or until slightly golden brown. Pour in 1 ½ cup of water and stir well. Bring it to a simmer and reduce the heat to low. Cook for 25-30 minutes, stirring occasionally. Remove from the heat and cover with a lid. Let it sit for 5 minutes.

Now, combine rice and onion mixture in a large bowl. Add tomatoes and cucumber. Sprinkle all with sherry vinegar, salt, and pepper to taste. Optionally, add some olive oil for extra flavor.

Finally, stir in the cheese, mint and parsley.

Serve immediately.

Nutritional information per serving: Kcal: 287, Protein: 7.1g, Carbs: 34.5g, Fats: 14.6g

13. Creamy Beet Salad

Ingredients:

6 oz. beets

1 egg, hard-boiled

½ cup Greek yogurt

2 tbsp. sour cream

2 tsp. yellow mustard

1 tbsp. fresh parsley, finely chopped

1 garlic clove, minced

2 walnuts, minced

2 tsp. pumpkin seeds

1 cup fresh arugula, roughly chopped

1 tbsp. olive oil

Salt

Preparation:

Trim off the green ends of the beets. Wash thoroughly and cut into thin slices. Place in a deep pot and add water enough to cover. Bring it to a boil over medium-high heat and cook for 15-20 minutes. Remove from the heat drain well. Set aside.

Heat up a non-stick skillet over medium-high heat. Add pumpkin seeds and stir-fry for 3-5 minutes, or until lightly toasted.

In a mixing bowl, combine Greek yogurt, sour cream, yellow mustard, and olive oil. Stir until combined and set aside.

Place the egg in a deep pot and add water enough to cover. Bring it to a boil over medium-high heat. Cook for 10-12 minutes. Remove from the heat and let it cool completely. Peel and chop into bite-sized pieces.

Now, combine beets, eggs, garlic, arugula, and pumpkin seeds. Add salt to taste and stir until well combined.

Pour over the yogurt mixture and stir once again before serving.

Enjoy!

Nutritional information per serving: Kcal: 265, Protein: 12.9g, Carbs: 13.7g, Fats: 19.1g

14. Lentil Tomato Salad

Ingredients:

1 cup lentils, drained

1 large Roma tomato, chopped

1 small Jalapeno pepper, finely chopped

1 garlic clove, minced

1 medium-sized cucumber, chopped

1 medium-sized purple onion, chopped

1 large red bell pepper, chopped

1 tbsp. olive oil

¼ tsp. cumin, ground

1 tbsp. lemon juice, freshly squeezed

Preparation:

Rinse the tomato and remove the stem. Chop into bite-sized pieces and set aside.

Wash the bell pepper and cut lengthwise in half. Remove the stem and seeds. Cut into bite-sized pieces and set aside.

Cut the cucumber into bite-sized pieces and set aside.

Peel the onion and chop into small pieces. Set aside.

Preheat the oil in a large saucepan over medium-high heat. Add garlic and Jalapeno pepper. Stir-fry for 2-3 minutes, or until golden.

Add lentils and sprinkle with cumin powder. Stir well and remove from the heat. Let it chill for a while and then transfer to a large bowl.

Now, add all vegetables to the bowl and drizzle with lemon juice. Toss to combine and serve immediately.

Nutritional information per serving: Kcal: 326, Protein: 18.8g, Carbs: 52.3g, Fats: 5.9g

15. Caesar Salad

Ingredients:

4 oz. chicken filets, skinless and boneless, cut into 1-inch thick strips

½ medium-sized tomato, chopped

1 egg, hard-boiled

¼ cup croutons

1 small cucumber, sliced

1 cup Iceberg lettuce

2 tbsp. Greek yogurt

1 tbsp. goat's cheese, crumbled

1 tbsp. olive oil

Salt and pepper to taste

Preparation:

Rinse the chicken under cold running water and pat-dry with a kitchen paper. Transfer to a cutting board and cut into bite-sized pieces. Set aside.

Preheat the oil in a medium saucepan over medium-high

heat. Add chicken and sprinkle with some salt and pepper to taste. Cook for 5 minutes, or until golden brown and crispy on the edges. Remove from the heat and set aside.

In a small mixing bowl, combine Greek yogurt, goat's cheese, olive oil, salt, and pepper. Mix until well combined and set aside.

Place the egg in a deep pot and add enough water to cover. Bring to a boil and cook for 12 minutes. Remove from the heat and rinse with ice cold water. Peel and chop into bite-sized pieces.

Now, combine chicken, tomato, croutons, cucumber, and lettuce in a large bowl. Drizzle with previously prepared dressing and stir well.

Serve immediately.

Nutritional information per serving: Kcal: 309, Protein: 15.7g, Carbs: 19g, Fats: 19.4g

16. Spicy Avocado Couscous Salad

Ingredients:

1 ripe avocado, cut into bite-sized pieces

½ cup couscous

1 tbsp. parsley, finely chopped

½ cup canned lentils, rinsed and drained

1 tbsp. canned corn, drained and rinsed

1 large red bell pepper, chopped

3 tbsp. olive oil

1 small chili pepper, seeded

1 garlic clove

½ tsp. salt

½ tsp. smoked paprika

Preparation:

Place the couscous in a deep bowl and pour in 1 cup of boiling water. Cover with a lid and let it stand for 10 minutes.

Meanwhile, combine olive oil, chili pepper, garlic, salt, and smoked paprika in a food processor. Blend until smooth and pureed. Optionally, add bell pepper instead chili if it is too spicy for your taste.

Fluff the couscous with a fork and add lentils along with avocado, corn, parsley, corn, and bell pepper.

Finally, drizzle with sauce and give it a good stir.

Serve immediately.

Nutritional information per serving: Kcal: 323, Protein: 9.3g, Carbs: 36.4g, Fats: 17g

17. Shiitake Spinach Salad

Ingredients:

1 cup Shiitake mushrooms, chopped

2 cups fresh baby spinach, roughly chopped

¼ cup Feta cheese, crumbled

1 garlic clove, minced

2 small beets, sliced

1 small onion, sliced

1 tsp. fresh thyme, ground

2 tbsp. olive oil

½ tbsp. balsamic vinegar

Salt and pepper to taste

Preparation:

Preheat the oil in a large saucepan over medium-high heat. Add garlic and onions. Stir-fry for 3-4 minutes, or until translucent.

Add mushrooms and sprinkle with some thyme, salt, and pepper to taste. Cook for 3-4 minutes, or until slightly soften.

Throw in the spinach and stir well. Cook for 2-3 minutes more and sprinkle with balsamic vinegar. Stir well and remove from the heat.

Transfer all to a large salad bowl and top with sliced beets, onions, and cheese.

Serve immediately.

Nutritional information per serving: Kcal: 278, Protein: 6.9g, Carbs: 26g, Fats: 18.5g

18. Potato Salad with Creamy Dressing

Ingredients:

2 medium-sized potatoes, cut into bite-sized pieces

1 large red bell pepper, chopped

1 small cucumber, sliced

¼ cup spring onions, chopped

1 tsp. yellow mustard

4 tbsp. Greek yogurt

1 tsp. white wine vinegar

¼ tsp. black pepper, ground

½ tsp. salt

Preparation:

Place the potatoes in a deep pot and add enough water to cover. Bring to a boil over medium-high heat. Cook for 10-15 minutes, or until fork-tender. Remove from the heat and drain. Set aside.

In a small mixing bowl, combine Greek yogurt, white wine vinegar, yellow mustard, black pepper, and salt. Mix until well combined and set aside.

Now, place the potatoes in a salad bowl and drizzle over with yogurt dressing. Sprinkle with green onions before serving.

Enjoy!

Nutritional information per serving: Kcal: 202, Protein: 6.5g, Carbs: 45.1g, Fats: 0.8g

19. Simple Tomato Mozzarella Salad

Ingredients:

2 large tomatoes, cut into bite-sized pieces

½ cup Mozzarella cheese, sliced

½ small purple onion, finely chopped

¼ cup olives, pitted

2 tbsp. fresh parsley, finely chopped

½ tsp. dried oregano, ground

1 tbsp. extra-virgin olive oil

¼ tsp. sea salt

¼ tsp. black pepper

Preparation:

Rinse the tomatoes and cut into bite-sized pieces. Transfer to a salad bowl and add mozzarella cheese.

In a small mixing bowl, combine olive oil, dried oregano, sea salt, and black pepper. Mix until combined.

Drizzle the prepared salad with the dressing.

Sprinkle with parsley and top with olives before serving.

Enjoy!

Nutritional information per serving: Kcal: 285, Protein: 8.2g, Carbs: 21.3g, Fats: 21g

20. Bean Salad With Feta and Chia Seeds

Ingredients:

½ cup canned beans, drained and rinsed

1 small red onion, chopped

1 garlic clove, finely chopped

1 large tomato, chopped

¼ cup Feta cheese, crumbled

4 tsp. chia seeds

1 tsp. shallots, finely chopped

1 tbsp. fresh parsley, finely chopped

1 tsp. apple cider vinegar

1 tsp. yellow mustard

2 tbsp. olive oil

¼ tsp. cumin, ground

¼ tsp. dried oregano, ground

½ tsp. salt

¼ tsp. black pepper, ground

Preparation:

In a small mixing bowl, combine olive oil, apple cider vinegar, garlic, cumin, oregano, salt and pepper. Mix until well combined and set aside.

Place the beans in a large colander. Rinse under cold running water. Drain and transfer to a serving bowl.

Add tomato and onion. Drizzle with previously prepared mixture and give it a good stir.

Sprinkle with chia seeds and serve immediately.

Enjoy!

Nutritional information per serving: Kcal: 218, Protein: 4.8g, Carbs: 11.1g, Fats: 18.6g

21. Pepper Salad with Lentils

Ingredients:

4 large red bell peppers

½ cup lentils, drained

1 tbsp. fresh parsley, finely chopped

1 tbsp. fresh basil, finely chopped

1 tsp. fresh mint, finely chopped

¼ cup Feta cheese, cut into small cubes

2 tsp. balsamic vinegar

2 tbsp. olive oil

¼ tsp. cumin, ground

2-3 walnuts, chopped

¼ tsp. cayenne pepper

Preparation:

Preheat one tablespoon of olive oil in a large skillet over medium-high heat. Add peppers and sprinkle with some salt to taste. Cook for 3-4 minutes on each side, or until tender.

Rinse the lentils using a colander. Drain well and set aside.

Now, combine the remaining oil, balsamic vinegar, cumin, cayenne pepper, parsley, basil, and mint in a mixing bowl. Stir until well combined.

Combine peppers, lentils, and Feta cheese on a serving dish. Drizzle all with previously prepared dressing.

Top with walnuts and serve immediately.

Enjoy!

Nutritional information per serving: Kcal: 218, Protein: 4.8g, Carbs: 11.1g, Fats: 18.6g

22. Carrot Mustard Salad

Ingredients:

4 large carrots

1 tsp. yellow mustard

1 tsp. lemon juice, freshly squeezed

1 tbsp. olive oil

2 tbsp. fresh parsley, finely chopped

¼ tsp. dried thyme, ground

Salt and pepper

Preparation:

Rinse the carrot and gently peel the outer skin. Cut into thin slices and transfer to a salad bowl. Set aside.

In a small mixing bowl, combine yellow mustard, lemon juice, olive oil, and thyme. Add salt and pepper according to your taste. Mix until combined and drizzle over the carrots.

Give it a good stir and let it stand for 30 minutes before serving.

Enjoy!

Nutritional information per serving: Kcal: 246, Protein: 2.9g, Carbs: 29.4g, Fats: 14.3g

23. Tuna Rice Salad

Ingredients:

½ brown rice

4 oz. minced tuna, drained

1 tbsp. orange juice, freshly squeezed

½ fresh lemon, juiced

1 tbsp. fresh parsley, finely chopped

½ tsp. Italian seasoning

1 tbsp. drained capers

¼ cup olives, chopped

¼ tsp. smoked paprika, ground

¼ tsp. salt

1 tbsp. olive oil

Preparation:

In a small mixing bowl, combine olive oil, Italian seasoning, capers, olives, smoked paprika, and salt.

Place the rice in a heavy-bottomed pot. Add 1 ½ cup of water and bring it to a boil over medium-high heat. Cook for about 10-15 minutes, or until almost all the liquid has been absorbed.

Add lemon juice and orange juice. Give it a good stir and remove from the heat. Set aside to chill completely.

Transfer the rice to a serving bowl and add tuna and parsley. Drizzle with previously prepared mixture and stir well.

Serve immediately.

Nutritional information per serving: Kcal: 370, Protein: 19.2g, Carbs: 40g, Fats: 15.1g

24. Broccoli Lentil Salad

Ingredients:

2 cups fresh broccoli, chopped

½ cup lentils, soaked overnight

¼ cup spring onions, chopped

2 tbsp. parsley, finely chopped

1 garlic clove, minced

1 tsp. Dijon mustard

1 tsp. maple syrup

1 tbsp. olive oil

1 tbsp. apple cider vinegar

¼ tsp. black pepper

½ salt

Preparation:

Drain the lentils and place in a deep pot. Add two cups of water and bring it to boil. Cook for 20 minutes. Remove from the heat and drain well. Set aside.

Rinse the broccoli under cold running water using a large

colander. Drain and chop into bite-sized pieces. Steam for 10 minutes, or until tender.

In a small mixing bowl, combine parsley, Dijon mustard, maple syrup, olive oil, apple cider vinegar, pepper, and salt. Mix until well combined.

In a large salad bowl, combine lentils and broccoli. Drizzle with previously prepared dressing and give it a good stir.

Serve immediately.

Nutritional information per serving: Kcal: 370, Protein: 19.2g, Carbs: 40g, Fats: 15.1g

25. Sesame Chicken Salad

Ingredients:

4 oz. chicken breast, skinless and boneless

½ small onion, chopped

2 tsp. soy sauce

½ tsp. dried rosemary, ground

½ cup cherry tomatoes, chopped

¼ cup cottage cheese

1 tsp. sesame seeds

1 tsp. balsamic vinegar

2 cups Romaine lettuce, roughly chopped

1 tbsp. olive oil

Salt to taste

Preparation:

Rinse the chicken under running water and pat-dry with a kitchen paper. Transfer to a cutting board and cut into strips. Generously brush with soy sauce and sprinkle with rosemary. Let it sit for 10 minutes to allow spices to penetrate into the meat.

Preheat the oil in a skillet over medium-high heat. Add chicken and cook for 5 minutes, or until golden brown.

In a large salad bowl, combine lettuce, cheese, and cherry tomatoes. Top with meat and sprinkle all with sesame seeds and balsamic vinegar.

Add some salt to taste. However it's optional.

Enjoy!

Nutritional information per serving: Kcal: 371, Protein: 34.7g, Carbs: 14.1g, Fats: 19.9g

26. Beet Salad with Leeks

Ingredients:

2 large beets, chopped into bite-sized pieces

1 cup leeks, chopped

1 large carrot, sliced

1 garlic clove, minced

1 cup Greek yogurt

½ tsp. dried thyme

½ whole lemon, juiced

½ tsp. black pepper

Salt

1 tbsp. olive oil

Preparation:

Rinse the beet well and trim off the green parts. Place it in a deep pot and add water enough to cover. Bring it to a boil and cook for 20 minutes. Remove from the heat and drain. Let it cool completely and chop into bite-sized pieces.

Preheat the oil in a skillet over medium-high heat. Add

carrots and cook for 5 minutes, stirring occasionally. Add leeks and garlic. Pour in some water to help the cooking process. Stir-fry for about 10-15 minutes, or until the leeks are tender.

In a small mixing bowl, combine Greek yogurt, lemon juice, thyme, pepper, and salt. Mix until well combined.

Now, combine cooked beets, carrots, and leeks in a salad bowl. Drizzle over with yogurt dressing and give it a good stir.

Serve immediately.

Nutritional information per serving: Kcal: 332, Protein: 25.8g, Carbs: 49.6g, Fats: 4.8g

27.   Sweet Potato Kale Salad with Sesame Seeds

Ingredients:

1 medium-sized sweet potato, chopped

2 cups fresh kale, chopped

1 tsp. apple cider vinegar

1 tsp. avocado oil

1 tsp. sesame seeds

1 garlic clove, minced

Salt and pepper to taste

Preparation:

Peel and wash the potato. Cut into bite-sized pieces and transfer to a large pot. Add water enough to cover and sprinkle with some salt. Bring to a boil over medium-high heat. Cook for 5 minutes and turn off the heat. Cover with a lid and let it stand in hot water.

Using a large colander, rinse the kale under running water. Drain and torn into small pieces.

Preheat the oil in a saucepan over medium-high heat. Add garlic and cook for 2-3 minutes. Now, add kale and continue to cook for 3-4 minutes, or until wilted. Remove from the heat and set aside.

In a large salad bowl, combine sweet potato and kale. Drizzle with apple cider vinegar and sprinkle with sesame seeds. Give it a good stir and serve immediately.

Nutritional information per serving: Kcal: 198, Protein: 7.1g, Carbs: 39.6g, Fats: 2.3g

28. Watercress Mango Salad with Pomegranate Seeds

Ingredients:

2 cups watercress, chopped

1 ripe mango, chopped

¼ cup pomegranate seeds

1 tbsp. walnuts, chopped

1 orange, freshly juiced

½ lemon, freshly juiced

3 tsp. hemp oil

1 tsp. honey

Salt and pepper to taste

Preparation:

Using a large colander, rinse the watercress under cold running water. Drain and set aside.

Peel the mango and chop into bite-sized pieces. Set aside.

In a small mixing bowl, combine orange juice, lemon juice, hemp oil, honey, salt, and pepper. Mix until well combined and set aside.

In a salad bowl, combine watercress and mango. Drizzle with previously prepared dressing and give it a good stir.

Top with pomegranate seeds and walnuts before serving.

Nutritional information per serving: Kcal: 198, Protein: 7.1g, Carbs: 39.6g, Fats: 2.3g

29. Spicy Orange Cumin Salad

Ingredients:

3 large oranges, peeled

1 small red onion, chopped

2 tsp. olive oil

¼ cup olives, pitted

1 whole lime, juiced

½ tsp. black pepper, ground

½ tsp. black cumin powder

Preparation:

Peel the orange and divide into wedges. Set aside.

Peel the onions and cut into thin slices along with olives.

In a small mixing bowl, combine lime juice, pepper, and cumin powder. Mix until well combined. Set aside.

Now, combine orange, onions, and olives in a salad bowl. Drizzle with previously prepared dressing.

Optionally, top with finely chopped coriander leaves or basil.

Serve immediately.

Nutritional information per serving: Kcal: 244, Protein: 3.2g, Carbs: 47.1g, Fats: 6.9g

30. Cauliflower Broccoli Salad with Dried Cranberries

Ingredients:

2 cups cauliflower, chopped

2 cups broccoli, chopped

1 tbsp. dried cranberries

1 tbsp. almond flakes

1 tsp. Dijon mustard

1 whole lemon, juiced

2 garlic cloves, minced

1 tsp. avocado oil

½ tsp. black pepper, ground

½ tsp. salt

Preparation:

Line a small baking sheet with some parchment paper. Spread the almond flakes evenly in one layer. Place it in the oven and bake for 2 minutes at 450 degrees. Remove from the oven and let it cool completely.

Rinse the cauliflower and broccoli using a large colander.

Chop into bite-sized pieces and place in a large bowl. Add cranberries and toasted almonds and set aside.

In a small mixing bowl, combine Dijon mustard, lemon juice, garlic, avocado oil, pepper, and salt. Mix until combined and drizzle the salad. Give it a good stir and serve immediately.

Enjoy!

Nutritional information per serving: Kcal: 291, Protein: 15.1g, Carbs: 29g, Fats: 14.7g

31. Creamy Tuna Tomato Salad

Ingredients:

1 large tomato, chopped

4 oz. canned tuna, drained

1 large green bell pepper, chopped

1 small cucumber, cubed

1 cup Greek yogurt

1 tsp. apple cider vinegar

1 tsp. pine nuts

1 tbsp. extra-virgin olive oil

Salt and pepper to taste

Preparation:

Wash the tomato and chop into bite-sized pieces. Place in a large salad bowl and set aside.

Cut the pepper lengthwise into halves. Remove the stem and seeds. Chop into small pieces and add to the bowl.

Wash the cucumber and cut into small cubes. Add to the bowl and set aside.

Now, combine yogurt, vinegar, pine nuts, and olive oil in a small mixing bowl. Add salt and pepper according to your taste and mix well.

Drizzle the creamy dressing over the salad and give it a good stir. Add more salt and pepper if needed.

Serve immediately.

Nutritional information per serving: Kcal: 309, Protein: 27.7g, Carbs: 17.7g, Fats: 15.1g

32. Grape Tomato Avocado Salad with Greek Dressing

Ingredients:

1 cup grape tomatoes, chopped

1 small cucumber, chopped

½ ripe avocado, chopped

1 small purple onion, sliced

½ cup Feta cheese, crumbled

1 tbsp. fresh parsley, finely chopped

2 tbsp. olive oil

½ whole lemon, juiced

1 tsp. Dijon mustard

1 garlic clove, crushed

1 tsp. fresh basil, finely chopped

¼ tsp. dried oregano, ground

Salt to taste

Preparation:

In a mixing bowl, combine olive oil, fresh lemon juice, Dijon mustard, garlic, fresh basil, oregano, and salt. Mix until well combined and set aside.

Wash cucumber and cut into thin slices. Set aside.

Using a large colander, rinse the grape tomatoes under running water. Drain and cut each in half. Set aside.

Cut the avocado in half. Remove the pit and cut into thin slices. Reserve the rest in the refrigerator. Optionally, sprinkle with some lemon juice and set aside for 5 minutes.

Peel the onion and chop into small pieces.

Now, combine tomatoes, cucumber, avocado, and onion in a salad bowl. Drizzle all with previously prepared dressing and give it a gentle stir. Sprinkle all with fresh parsley and serve immediately.

Nutritional information per serving: Kcal: 253, Protein: 5.8g, Carbs: 12.6g, Fats: 21.5g

33. Smoked Trout Fusilli Salad

Ingredients:

3 oz. fusilli pasta

2 oz. smoked trout, thinly sliced

½ cup sour cream

2 large red bell peppers, chopped

½ tsp. dried dill, ground

½ whole lemon, juiced

1 tbsp. olive oil

Salt and pepper to taste

Preparation:

Place the pasta in a deep pot and water enough to cover. Bring to a boil over medium-high heat. Cook for 10-13 minutes. Remove from the heat and drain using a large colander. Rinse under cold running water and set aside.

Cut the bell peppers lengthwise into halves. Remove the stems and seeds. Chop into small pieces and set aside.

In a small bowl, combine sour cream, lemon juice, olive oil, salt, and pepper. Mix until well combined.

In a salad bowl, combine pasta, smoked trout, and bell peppers. Drizzle with prepared dressing and gently stir.

Optionally, garnish with some fresh parsley, or add a few olives before serving.

Enjoy!

Nutritional information per serving: Kcal: 288, Protein: 10.8g, Carbs: 29g, Fats: 14.9g

34. Mexican Potato Salad

Ingredients:

2 large potatoes, cut into cubes

1 large red bell pepper, chopped

¼ cup cheddar cheese, shredded

2 tbsp. red wine vinegar

1 tbsp. corn, rinsed and drained

½ cup spring onions, chopped

1 tbsp. fresh parsley, finely chopped

¼ cup Greek yogurt

2 tbsp. olive oil

½ whole lime, juiced

½ tsp. garlic powder

1 tsp. dried oregano, ground

¼ tsp. cumin powder

¼ tsp. chili powder

½ tsp. black pepper, ground

Salt

Preparation:

In a mixing bowl, combine Greek yogurt, olive oil, lime juice, garlic powder, oregano, cumin, chili powder, salt, and pepper. Mix until well combined and refrigerate.

Peel and wash the potatoes. Place in a deep pot and sprinkle with some salt. Add water enough to cover and bring to a boil over medium-high heat. Cook for 20 minutes, or until tender. Remove from the heat and drain. Set aside to cool completely. Chop into bite-sized cubes and set aside.

In a small bowl, combine salt and red wine vinegar. Mix until the salt has been dissolved. Drizzle over the potatoes and give it a good stir and set aside until all the liquid has been soaked up.

Now, add bell peppers and shredded cheddar cheese. Drizzle all with previously prepared yogurt mixture and gently stir.

Serve immediately.

Nutritional information per serving: Kcal: 278, Protein: 8.1g, Carbs: 40.9g, Fats: 10.4g

35.   Eggplant Chermoula Salad

Ingredients:

2 medium-sized eggplants, sliced

2 tbsp. olive oil

1 garlic clove, minced

½ tsp. cumin powder

½ tsp. coriander powder

½ tsp. smoked paprika

1 tbsp. fresh parsley, finely chopped

1 tbsp. fresh cilantro, finely chopped

¼ cup fresh spring onions, chopped

1 tbsp. lemon juice, freshly squeezed

Salt

Preparation:

Preheat the oven to 400 degrees. Line some parchment paper over a baking sheet and set aside.

Rinse well the eggplants and pat-dry with a kitchen paper. Transfer to a cutting board and cut into thin slices using a sharp knife.

Spread the eggplant over a prepared baking sheet and bake for 20-25 minutes.

When done, remove from the oven and let it cool completely.

In a food processor, combine olive oil, garlic, cumin powder, coriander powder, smoked paprika, parsley, cilantro, spring onions, fresh lemon juice, and salt. Pulse until well incorporated.

Transfer the chilled eggplant to a serving dish and drizzle over with chermoula dressing.

Optionally, serve with some garlic toasted bread.

Enjoy!

Nutritional information per serving: Kcal: 269, Protein: 6g, Carbs: 34.5g, Fats: 15.3g

36. Zucchini Carpaccio Salad

Ingredients:

3 medium-sized zucchinis, thinly sliced

¼ cup Parmesan cheese, thinly sliced

2 tbsp. capers, drained

¼ cup black olives

1 whole lemon, freshly juiced

½ cup fresh mint, roughly chopped

3 tbsp. olive oil

1 tsp. apple cider vinegar

Salt and pepper to taste

Preparation:

Rinse and pat-dry the zucchinis. Using a sharp paring knife, cut thin lengthwise slices. Discard the middle parts with seeds.

Spread the zucchini slices in one layer over a large baking sheet. Sprinkle with salt, pepper, and vinegar. Set aside for 30 minutes.

Now, in a small mixing bowl, combine olive oil, lemon juice, salt, and pepper. Mix until well combined.

Transfer the zucchini to a serving bowl and drizzle with previously prepared dressing. Top with mint, capers, and cheese.

Stir once and serve immediately.

Enjoy!

Nutritional information per serving: Kcal: 304, Protein: 9.2g, Carbs: 13.8g, Fats: 26.6g

37. Roquefort Radish Salad with Raspberries

Ingredients:

2 cups fresh arugula, chopped

3 medium-sized radishes, sliced

½ cup Roquefort cheese, (or any other blue cheese you have on hand)

½ cup fresh raspberries

1 tbsp. walnuts, finely chopped

1 tbsp. olive oil

1 tsp. apple cider vinegar

¼ tsp. dried dill, ground

Salt and pepper

Preparation:

Using a large colander, rinse the arugula under cold running water. Drain and roughly torn with your hands. Transfer to a large salad bowl and set aside. Optionally, sprinkle with some lemon juice for some extra flavor.

Rinse the radishes and trim off the green parts. Cut into thin slices and add to the bowl with arugula.

Cut the cheese into small cubes and add to the salad.

Now, sprinkle all with olive oil, apple cider vinegar, dried dill, and salt. Give it a good stir and top with raspberries and walnuts.

Serve immediately.

Nutritional information per serving: Kcal: 226, Protein: 9.1g, Carbs: 5.8g, Fats: 19.3g

38. Asparagus Strawberry Salad

Ingredients:

5 oz. asparagus, trimmed and chopped

6 oz. strawberries, chopped

¼ cup raspberries

1 tbsp. balsamic vinegar

1 tbsp. olive oil

Salt and pepper

Preparation:

In a food processor, combine raspberries, balsamic vinegar, olive oil, salt, and pepper. Pulse until smooth and set aside.

Rinse and drain the asparagus. Trim off the woody ends and cut into bite-sized pieces. Transfer to a deep pot and add enough water to cover. Bring to a boil over medium-high heat. Cook for 2 minutes and remove from the heat. Drain and set aside to cool completely.

Using a large colander, rinse well the strawberries. Drain and remove the stems. Chop into bite-sized pieces.

Now, combine asparagus and strawberries in a large bowl.

Drizzle with previously prepared sauce and give it a good stir.

Serve immediately.

Nutritional information per serving: Kcal: 222, Protein: 4.6g, Carbs: 22.4g, Fats: 14.9g

39. Creamy Cucumber Salad

Ingredients:

2 cups Greek yogurt

2 medium-sized cucumbers, finely chopped

2 garlic cloves, minced

¼ cup fresh dill, finely chopped

2 tbsp. extra-virgin olive oil

1 tbsp. walnuts, finely chopped

Salt and pepper to taste

Preparation:

Wash the cucumbers and chop into small pieces. Place in a large salad bowl and set aside.

In a small bowl, garlic, fresh dill, olive oil, salt, and pepper. Mix until well incorporated and pour over the cucumbers. Mix once and set aside for 15 minutes to allow flavors to merge.

Now, add Greek yogurt and stir until all well combined. Top with walnuts before serving.

Optionally, add some cayenne pepper or chili for some

extra flavor.

Enjoy!

Nutritional information per serving: Kcal: 360, Protein: 24.5g, Carbs: 23.7g, Fats: 20.9g

40. Greek Lentil Salad

Ingredients:

½ cup lentils, soaked overnight

1 small purple onion, chopped

1 small cucumber, chopped

½ cup cherry tomatoes, halved

¼ cup Kalamata olives

¼ cup Feta cheese, cubed

1 tsp. fresh dill, finely chopped

2 tbsp. olive oil

1 garlic clove, crushed

¼ tsp. dried oregano, ground

1 tbsp. lemon juice, freshly squeezed

Salt and pepper to taste

Preparation:

In a small mixing bowl, combine olive oil, garlic, dried oregano, lemon juice, salt, and pepper. Mix until well combined and set aside.

Drain the lentils and place in a deep pot. Add 2 cups of water and a pinch of salt. Bring to a boil over medium-high heat. Cook for 20 minutes and remove from the heat. Drain well and rinse under cold water to chill. Set aside.

Wash and prepare the vegetables.

In a large salad bowl, combine onions, cucumber, cherry tomatoes, Kalamata olives, and Feta cheese. Add lentils and stir once.

Now, drizzle with previously prepared dressing and stir well.

Serve immediately.

Nutritional information per serving: Kcal: 273, Protein: 11.5g, Carbs: 28.1g, Fats: 13.8g

41. Broccoli Salad with Raisins

Ingredients:

2 cups broccoli, chopped

1 small purple onion, finely chopped

1 tbsp. raisins

½ cup cheddar cheese, cut into cubes

½ cup cherry tomatoes, halved

2 tsp. apple cider vinegar

1 tbsp. olive oil

Salt and pepper

Preparation:

Using a large colander, rinse the broccoli under cold running water. Chop into bite-sized pieces and set aside.

Peel the onion and finely chop. Set aside.

Rinse the cherry tomatoes and remove the stems. Cut each tomato in half and set aside. In case you use the regular tomato, remove the seeds and cut into small pieces.

Now, combine broccoli, onion, tomatoes, raisins, and

cheddar cheese in a large salad bowl. Sprinkle all with apple cider vinegar, olive oil, salt, and pepper.

Mix until all well incorporated and serve immediately.

Nutritional information per serving: Kcal: 242, Protein: 10.5g, Carbs: 15.1g, Fats: 16.8g

42. Classic Waldorf Salad

Ingredients:

2 large Granny Smith's apple, cored

2 large celery sticks

1 cup Greek yogurt

½ whole lemon, juiced

1 tbsp. walnuts, minced

Salt and pepper to taste

Parsley

Preparation:

Wash the apples and cut lengthwise in half. Remove the core and cut into thin slices or strips. Set aside.

Rinse the celery and discard the leaves. Cut each stick into 1-inch thick strips. Set aside.

In a mixing bowl, combine Greek yogurt, lemon, salt, and pepper. Mix until well incorporated and set aside.

Now, combine apples and celery in a salad bowl. Add yogurt mixture and stir until all well combined.

Top with walnuts and garnish with parsley.

Enjoy!

Nutritional information per serving: Kcal: 226, Protein: 11.6g, Carbs: 37.2g, Fats: 4.7g

43. Green Bean Fusilli Salad

Ingredients:

4 oz. fusilli pasta

1 cup green beans

¼ cup Feta cheese, crumbled

¼ cup olives, pitted and chopped

2 garlic cloves, minced

½ onion, finely chopped

1 cup yogurt, low-fat

1 tsp. yellow mustard

2 tbsp. olive oil

½ tsp. dried dill, ground

½ tsp. red pepper, ground

Salt

Preparation:

Place the pasta in a deep pot. Add enough water to cover and bring it to a boil. Sprinkle with some salt and cook for 10 minutes over medium-high heat. Remove from the heat and transfer to a large colander. Rinse under cold running water and set aside.

Place the green beans in a deep pot and cover with water. Bring to a boil over medium-high heat and cook for 5 minutes. Remove from the heat and drain. Set aside.

Preheat one tablespoon of olive oil in a large skillet over medium-high heat. Add onions and garlic. Stir-fry for 2-3 minutes, or until translucent. Add green beans and cook for 5 minutes. Remove from the heat and transfer to a large salad bowl.

Add pasta to the bowl and stir well. Set aside.

Now, combine the remaining olive oil, yogurt, mustard, dried dill, red pepper, and a pinch of salt in a mixing bowl. Mix until well combined and pour over prepared beans and pasta. Top with olives and cheese before serving.

Enjoy!

Nutritional information per serving: Kcal: 264, Protein: 9.3g, Carbs: 31.5g, Fats: 11.2g

44. Cooked Celery Salad

Ingredients:

4 celery sticks, with leaves

1 whole lemon, juiced

3 tbsp. walnuts, halved

1 small purple onion, finely chopped

2 tbsp. white wine vinegar

2 cups lamb's lettuce, roughly chopped

1 tsp. flaxseed oil

½ tsp. salt

½ tsp. black pepper, ground

Preparation:

Rinse the celery under cold running water and drain. Transfer to a cutting board and separate sticks and leaves. Chop the sticks into strips and finely chop the leaves. Set aside.

Transfer the celery sticks in a deep pot. Cover with water and bring to a boil over medium-high heat. Cook for 8 minutes. Add celery leaves and fresh lemon juice. Stir once and cook for 2-3 minutes more. Remove from the heat and drain. Rinse all under cold running water immediately. Set aside.

In a mixing bowl, combine onions, vinegar, salt, and pepper. Mix until well incorporated. Add flaxseed oil and mix again until combined.

Now, arrange the lamb's lettuce over a serving dish and top with celery. Drizzle with previously prepared dressing.

Serve cold.

Nutritional information per serving: Kcal: 273, Protein: 8.8g, Carbs: 17.9g, Fats: 19g

45. Avocado Egg Salad

Ingredients:

1 ripe avocado, cut into cubes

2 large eggs, hard-boiled

2 spring onions, chopped

½ cup Greek yogurt

1 tbsp. sour cream

1 whole lime, juiced

1 tsp. fresh thyme, finely chopped

Salt and pepper to taste

Preparation:

Place the eggs in a deep pot. Add water enough to cover and bring to a boil over medium-high heat. Cook for 10-12 minutes. Remove from the heat and transfer to a bowl with ice cold water. You can add a few ice cubes to speed up the process. Peel and cut into bite-sized pieces. Set aside.

Peel the avocado and cut lengthwise in half. Remove the pit and cut into bite-sized cubes. Set aside.

In a mixing bowl, combine Greek yogurt, sour cream, lime

juice, thyme, salt, and pepper. Mix until combined.

In a serving bowl, combine eggs and avocado. Drizzle with previously prepared dressing and give it a good stir.

Serve immediately.

Nutritional information per serving: Kcal: 343, Protein: 14g, Carbs: 16.3g, Fats: 27g

46. Grilled Mustard Turkey Salad

Ingredients:

8 oz. turkey breast, skinless and boneless

1 tbsp. yellow mustard

3 tsp. olive oil

½ tsp. salt

½ tsp. black pepper, ground

2 cups Romaine lettuce, chopped

1 cup lamb's lettuce

½ cup cherry tomatoes, chopped

1 tbsp. Parmesan cheese, shredded

2 tsp. red wine vinegar

Preparation:

Rinse and drain the turkey breast. Transfer to a cutting board and cut into thin slices. Set aside.

In a small mixing bowl, combine 2 teaspoons of olive oil, salt, black pepper, and mustard. Mix until combined and pour over the meat. Rub with your hands to allow flavors to penetrate into the meat. Cover the dish with a plastic foil and refrigerate for 1 hour.

Preheat the grill to medium-high. Add meat and grill for 3-4 minutes on each side. Remove from the heat and transfer to a cutting board. Let it chill for a while and then cut into strips.

Wash and prepare the vegetables.

In a large salad bowl, combine lettuce, lamb's lettuce, and cherry tomatoes. Top with turkey strips and drizzle with red wine vinegar. Sprinkle with parmesan cheese and serve immediately.

Nutritional information per serving: Kcal: 248, Protein: 25g, Carbs: 9.6g, Fats: 12.4g

47. Shrimp Avocado Salad

Ingredients:

4 oz. shrimps, cleaned and deveined

½ ripe avocado, chopped

¼ cup Feta cheese, crumbled

1 medium-sized green bell pepper, chopped

½ cup cherry tomatoes, chopped

½ cup fresh mint, roughly chopped

1 small purple onion, chopped

¼ cup green olives, pitted

1 tbsp. fresh parsley, finely chopped

1 whole lime, juiced

¼ tsp. garlic powder

¼ tsp. dried oregano, ground

½ tsp. red pepper flakes

2 tbsp. olive oil

Salt to taste

Preparation:

In a small mixing bowl, combine lime juice, oregano, garlic, 1 tablespoon of olive oil, pepper flakes, and salt. Mix until well combined and set aside.

Wash and prepare the vegetables.

In a large salad bowl, combine cherry tomatoes, mint, purple onion, green olives, and parsley. Drizzle with previously prepared dressing and refrigerate for 20 minutes.

Preheat the remaining oil in a skillet over medium-high heat. Add shrimps and sprinkle with some salt and red pepper. Cook for 2-3 minutes, or until set. Remove from the heat and set aside to chill for a while.

Now, add cheese and avocado to the salad. Mix again and top with shrimps. Garnish with fresh mint and serve immediately.

Enjoy!

Nutritional information per serving: Kcal: 264, Protein: 12.6g, Carbs: 12.2g, Fats: 19.6g

ADDITIONAL TITLES FROM THIS AUTHOR

70 Effective Meal Recipes to Prevent and Solve Being Overweight: Burn Fat Fast by Using Proper Dieting and Smart Nutrition

By

Joe Correa CSN

48 Acne Solving Meal Recipes: The Fast and Natural Path to Fixing Your Acne Problems in Less Than 10 Days!

By

Joe Correa CSN

41 Alzheimer's Preventing Meal Recipes: Reduce or Eliminate Your Alzheimer's Condition in 30 Days or Less!

By

Joe Correa CSN

70 Effective Breast Cancer Meal Recipes: Prevent and Fight Breast Cancer with Smart Nutrition and Powerful Foods

By

Joe Correa CSN